THE ƒoundling MUSEUM

Contents

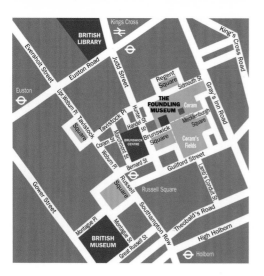

Contents

Author | Kit Wedd
Editor | Rhian Harris / Lars Tharp
Photographer | Richard Bryant
Designer | Tim Harvey
Printer | BAS Printers
© The Foundling Museum, 2004 / 2009
Publisher | The Foundling Museum

The Foundling Museum
40 Brunswick Square
London WC1N 1AZ
Telephone 020 7841 3600
Fax 020 7841 3601
www.foundlingmuseum.org.uk

Open | Tuesday–Saturday 10am–5pm
Sunday 11–5pm

Times may vary over public holiday periods. Please
check the Foundling Museum website for changes
www.foundlingmuseum.org.uk

Registered charity no.1071167

front cover
William Hogarth (1697–1764)
Captain Thomas Coram, **1740 (detail)**

back cover
**Boys marching out of the Foundling Hospital for the
last time in 1926
A mother's token from the collection**

ISBN 978-0-9551808-5-2

SUPPORTED BY THE
NATIONAL HERITAGE
MEMORIAL FUND

THE PRINTING OF THIS CATALOGUE
HAS BEEN GENEROUSLY SUPPORTED BY
JAMIE KORNER (MUSEUM TRUSTEE)
AND BY JULIA KORNER

Introduction

The last thing on Thomas Coram's mind would have been a museum. In 1722, at the age of fifty-four, he began a one-man campaign which, seventeen years later bore fruit with the establishment of Britain's first Hospital for the Maintenance and Education of Exposed and Deserted Young Children. From 1739 to 1953, Coram's socially enlightened venture was known as The Foundling Hospital.

Today the word "foundling" ("a child of unknown parentage, abandoned by its mother") seems quaint, endearing even; most of us are unaware of the very real stigma carried by the word until very recent times. Nowadays, occurrences of babies left on doorsteps or in telephone booths in our own country are rare and make the national news headlines. But in eighteenth century London the instances of abandoned babies and of infanticide were common - and on the increase. In such times, and even into the 20th century, to be a foundling was to be the personification of Sin - and therefore of Shame.

Seeing that the only provision for such babies in early Georgian London was the parish nurse, where survival rates among infants were almost zero (hence their being known as "killing nurses"), Thomas Coram realised that Something Had to Be Done. His often difficult experiences as a pioneer shipwright in Massachusetts, his championing of just causes and his tireless petitioning for worthy colonial projects already marked Coram as a man of principle and dogged determination. He now decided to create an institution intended to forestall the abandonment of babies; mothers unable to cope with a new-born infant would find a haven for the child to be reared before the darker alternatives crossed their thoughts. Such a refuge – a "hospital" in the old sense – would serve two purposes: the preservation of the child and, for the mother, the potential of respectability regained.

How Thomas Coram achieved his hospital, how it fared across three centuries and how his original purposes evolved and continue with the ongoing work of today's charity Coram – these are the themes which constitute the core of our young museum.

What Coram could never have predicted was how his "darling project" developed. Owing to the early involvement of the artist William Hogarth (himself on the threshold of his most successful decade) the Foundling Hospital soon became Britain's first indoor public art gallery and the seed-bed of today's Royal Academy; and shortly thereafter, with the equally active involvement of George Frideric Handel, the Hospital became fashionable for its music, becoming intimately bound up with the success of Handel's Messiah. The fortuitous convergence of these three strands – Childcare, Art and Music – left a unique and lasting legacy wholly unforeseen by Coram back in 1739 when George II granted the hospital its charter.

These strands are reflected today in the regular election of Foundling Fellows; in our regular programme of exhibitions covering Childhood, History and Contemporary art as well as a vibrant programme of concerts and the revival of a Foundling Choir.

By the 1990s Coram's charity, whose original mission was with the living and with the present, had also become a repository of its past – a unique collection of art and artefacts as well as an unparalleled archive of its own genesis. The latter can today be found at the London Metropolitan Archive. But how could the ongoing charity also act as a museum? Once more, Something

Had to be Done. A wholly new charity, today's Foundling Museum, was formed, charged with maintaining and displaying the Collection, and with ensuring it that remains intact, ultimately secured against any potential threat of dispersal or sale, however hypothetical. Meanwhile, unencumbered its curatrial burden, the Hospital's original philanthropic mission is free to continue and thrive under today's banner, Coram.

The Museum was established by a legal ruling from the Attorney-General, giving us twenty-five years in which to raise funds equivalent to the market value of the collection, effectively to "purchase" the collection from Coram. In this way two good deeds are accomplished in one act: the title of the works pass in perpetuity to the Museum while the monies raised are passed over to the charity. Works once freely given to the Hospital work for a second time.

Our collection is more valuable than the sum of its parts: it encapsulates a key moment in British social and philanthropic history; and it represents the lives and work of artists and friends. Above all, though, we reach into the lives of over twenty-five thousand children, their mothers, their foster-families and – in the shades – their fathers.

As I write, we are embarked on an exciting oral history project which, with the invaluable support of the Heritage Lottery Fund and the assistance of the Old Coram Association as well as from Coram itself, seeks to record the lives of former pupils of the Hospital. The most senior of our participants are in their high nineties and can recall the hospital before is removal from Bloomsbury in 1926. Their often poignant testimonies become an invaluable part of our permanent Collection and I hope you will revisit us as more of their voices are brought forward in these rooms in the years ahead.

Finally, I should like to thank all those generous benefactors and trustees who, since the late 1990s and under the inspired guidance of Patrick Walker as well as our first director, Rhian Harris (my predecessor), launched this, London's most remarkable museum. My thanks go also to our highly dedicated trustees, today under the chairmanship of Alan Borg. In particular I must thank Jamie and Julia Korner for making it possible to reprint this little guide, proceeds from which go straight to the Museum's ever-ongoing fund-raising campaign.

The clock of the twenty-five year moratorium is ticking. Like Coram himself, we have a big but achievable challenge. If you would like in some way to follow in the footsteps of those first subscribers and legatees, and maybe to join our "1739" benefactors' circle, I should be delighted to hear from you.

Meanwhile, welcome to the Foundling Museum.

Director

The Foundling Hospital

'A Hospital for the Maintenance and Education of Exposed and Deserted Young Children'

The streets of London in the 1720s presented startling contrasts of wealth and poverty, respectability and debauchery, fashionable extravagance and utter destitution. One of the most appalling symptoms of poverty was the large number of babies who were abandoned in the streets, on the steps of churches and workhouses, and even on dungheaps, throughout the capital.

Desperate parents who could not care for their babies had little choice but to abandon them. Official provision for pauper children was scanty and depended on local parish funds or private charity. The Poor Rate—a charge levied by each parish for housing and feeding the poor—was much resented by respectable ratepayers, and officials were reluctant to add to the numbers of paupers they supported 'on the parish'.

Even if the parish officers accepted responsibility for a child, they did little to nurture it. Conditions in some workhouses were so bad that the infant mortality rate was 100%. A pauper child might fare no better outside the workhouse: parish nurses, who were paid to foster infants in their own homes, were sometimes known as 'killing-nurses' because so few of their charges survived.

It has been estimated that in the early eighteenth century as many as a thousand babies a year were abandoned in London alone. Such large numbers of discarded children were an embarrassment to a proud and prosperous nation. In Paris, abandoned babies had been cared for in the *Hôpital des Enfans-Trouvés* since 1670, and there were similar institutions in Lisbon, Florence, Rome, Venice, Vienna, Copenhagen and Amsterdam. Yet

Balthasar Nebot
(fl. 1737–1762),
Captain Coram
(Current whereabouts
unknown)

in Britain there was a deep reluctance to provide for foundlings.

This was due as much to prejudice as to meanness. Abandoned babies were tainted with the stigma of illegitimacy. As living proof of its parents' sin, an illegitimate child was morally suspect. As evidence of female unchastity, it destroyed the only asset that a poor woman could trade in the labour or marriage market—her respectable character. To nurture it would threaten the social order: if illegitimate children were not scorned, what incentive was there to enter into respectable marriage? And if bastards received the same treatment as legitimate offspring, what would prevent their claiming the same inheritance rights as legitimate heirs?

It would require a philanthropist of extraordinary vision and conviction to challenge these entrenched attitudes and show how basic humanity and common sense could be applied to the problem of caring for helpless and abandoned babies.

Captain Thomas Coram

Thomas Coram was born in about 1668 in the Dorset village of Lyme Regis and was sent to sea when he was 11 years old. At 16, he was apprenticed to a shipwright in London and by his mid-twenties he had done so well in the trade that he was ready to try his luck in the American colonies. In 1693 he travelled with a team of shipwrights to Boston, Massachusetts, intending to set up a shipyard. As a staunch member of the Church of England, he was regarded with suspicion by the Puritan New Englanders, and when he tried to expand his business on the river in the new settlement of Taunton, outside the relatively sophisticated society of Boston, he met outright hostility. So in 1702 Coram returned to

Boston, where he launched a lawsuit to try to reclaim some of his lost investment.

His court case failed and, six years after he had begun his American adventures, Coram returned to England thoroughly disheartened, except in one respect: in 1700 he had married Eunice Waite, the gentle, religiously-inclined daughter of a Congregationalist family in Boston. He remained happily married to his 'vertuous kind and Prudent Wife' until her death in 1740.

Back home, Coram embarked on his first philanthropic project, a plan to set up a colony in Massachusetts for destitute ex-soldiers. Between 1713 and 1720 he struggled to promote the scheme and was convinced that it failed only because the Massachusetts Agent played 'a trick on me to save that fine country for the villainous people of New England.' Later, a Trustee for the Colony of Georgia, he also campaigned for inheritance rights for daughters of colonists and land rights for Mohicans— unfashionable causes that illustrate his sympathy for the underdog and his willingness to battle against prejudice.

Childless himself, Coram loved children and found it easy to befriend them. 'I carry the Children a few apples, and sometimes give them a few plumbs,' he wrote of his visits to a poor emigrant family: 'a pound of malaga Raisins which costs 3d fille them with above 5 pounds worth of Love for me. They shew it by a Dawn of Joy in their faces as soon as they see me coming.'

In 1720 Coram was semi-retired and living on the outskirts of London. Business occasionally took him into the City, where he was appalled by the sight of young children 'exposed, sometimes alive, sometimes dead, and sometimes dying' at the roadside. He made up his mind to do something about it. By 1722 he had formed the idea of setting up an institution dedicated to the care and education of foundlings, and was starting to canvass support. A lesser man would have given up in the face of the obstacles he encountered. But Coram was energetic and persistent, and would not take no for an answer.

Coram the campaigner

An old enemy from New England had once testified in court that Coram was 'a man of that obstinate, persevering temper, as never to desist from his first enterprise, whatever obstacles lie in his way.' That 'temper' was to be sorely tested over the 17 years it took to make the Foundling Hospital a reality. In this context a 'Hospital' was not a medical institution, but a place where food and shelter were offered, and the Foundling Hospital would be an entirely new venture. Unlike previous attempts by church and government to care for the destitute in monasteries and workhouses, and unlike the orphanages run by the Catholic church in continental Europe, this was to be an entirely independent, secular charity. No such institution had ever existed before, so Coram had to start from scratch.

He turned lobbyist in order to persuade influential people of the need for a Foundling Hospital supported by donations and subscriptions. He began by 'making it the Topic of his Conversation, that he might learn the Sentiments of other Men; and from Thence form some Notion, whether what he had in view was practicable.' He needed to petition the King for a Charter of Incorporation, but had no idea how to approach the monarch. Lowly-born and newly-returned from America, Coram was barely on the margins of polite society and he found it impossible to gain

Detail of *Gin Lane* by William Hogarth and Thomas Coram's petition to 'Several Noble Lords and Gentlemen', *Coram's Children* exhibition

the support of anyone at court:

> ... for I could no more prevaile on any Arch Bishop or Bishop or Nobleman Britain or Foreigner or any other Great man, I tryed them all, to speake to the Late King or his present Majesty on this affair than I could have prevailed with any of them, if I had tryed it, to have putt down their Breeches and present their Backsides to the King and Queen in a full Drawing room such was the unchristian Shyness of all about the Court.

Coram 'bethought himself at last of applying to the Ladies', and found that women were the key to the hearts—and purses—of the great and good. Amongst society ladies, charity and benevolence, as well as a sentimental interest in motherhood and childhood, were becoming fashionable. In 1729 the Duchess of Somerset allowed herself to be persuaded to sign Coram's petition. Her example was followed by other noblewomen, many of whom were related by blood or by marriage; the Ladies' Petition is an early example of philanthropic networking.

Not all the women Coram approached could overcome their prejudices. He complained that 'Many weak persons, more Ladies than Gentlemen, say such a foundation will be a promotion of Wickedness'. As well as the almost universal contempt for illegitimate children, there were specific objections to the idea of a Foundling Hospital. Malicious gossips sniped that Coram and his supporters were hypocrites, hoping to dispose of their own illegitimate offspring whilst appearing to do good works. Moralists feared that providing for unwanted children would promote debauchery, or encourage feckless parents to expect others to pay for their children. Donations to the Hospital from 'well disposed

The Charter of Incorporation, which gave royal assent to the proposal to build 'the Hospital for the Maintenance and Education of Exposed and Deserted Young Children'

Citizens', they complained, would merely 'save the pockets of Whoremasters and other fornicating criminals'.

The Ladies' Petition to the King was crucial to Coram's eventual success. In 1734 he started collecting the signatures of prominent noblemen and gentlemen, including Dr Richard Mead, the King's physician. The following year he extended his petition to JPs in or near London and other 'Persons of Distinction'. Signatories were selected because of their social position, their unimpeachable respectability and their wealth. Coram travelled on foot all over London to collect signatures, claiming that he could easily walk 10 or 12 miles a day well into his seventies.

Finally, on 17 October 1739, George II signed the Charter officially incorporating the Hospital for the 'Maintenance and Education of Exposed and Deserted Young Children'.

Coram ensured the success of his project by choosing a board of Governors with 'the means to support it, the influence to promote it and the power to protect it'. No clergy were invited, except for the Archbishops of Canterbury and York and the Bishop of London, who were included by virtue of their offices. This reflects the secular nature of the undertaking, and may also indicate Coram's decision not to embarrass his clergy acquaintances by asking them to support a project that would have appalled many of their parishioners. The Governors held their first meeting in November 1739, in a room above the Crown and Anchor pub in the Strand.

Coram ousted

Just as his years of campaigning were beginning to bear fruit, Coram's association with the Hospital came to a sudden, sad end.

The Eastern Colonnade of the Foundling Hospital. This section still remains and is part of Coram's Fields. The colonnades gave shelter and also served as rope-walks.

In 1741, the year the first Foundlings were admitted to the Hospital, Coram was ousted from the Board of Governors by a boardroom *coup*. It seems that, in his usual bluff and forthright way, he had criticised two of his fellow Governors and some of the newly-appointed staff. Embarrassed by this public discussion of their private business, and afraid of attracting adverse comment before they had even begun their controversial work, the Governors closed ranks against their outspoken founder. By failing to elect him onto any of the committees appointed to build and run the Hospital, they froze him out of the administration of the institution he had created.

This was the inevitable price of respectability—and therefore success—for the Hospital scheme. Coram was an outsider in the company he had assembled. The very qualities that made him such a marvellous lobbyist—single-mindedness, persistence and blunt determination to overcome obstacles by the most direct route—made him a hopeless committee man. He lacked guile and had no patience with office politics or correct procedure. Not a gentleman, and still less an aristocrat, he was always going to be a potential embarrassment to men whose public reputation was dearer to them than anything else. He had to go.

Coram's only subsequent contact with the Hospital was at baptisms—he stood godfather to more than 20 Foundlings—and on private visits. Towards the end of his life he was often observed sitting in the Hospital's colonnade, somewhat shabbily dressed, 'distributing with tears in his Eyes Gingerbread to the Children'. On 29 March 1751 Captain Coram died at his lodgings near Leicester Square. In accordance with his own wishes, he was buried beneath the altar of the Hospital Chapel.

Harry Nelson O'Neil
(1817–1884)
*A Mother depositing
her child at the
Foundling Hospital in
Paris*

The first Foundlings

In 1741, having secured the lease of a house in Hatton Garden to
serve as temporary premises until a permanent Hospital building
could be built, the Governors issued a public notice:

'The governors give notice, that on Wednesday, the 25th
March, at 8 o'clock at night, and from that time till the House
should be full, their House will be opened for the reception of
Children ... no questions whatsoever shall be asked of any
person bringing a child, nor shall any servant of the Hospital
presume to discover who such person is, on pain of being
dismissed.'

In a society that prized 'good character' above all other feminine
virtues, the promise of anonymity was vital. The knowledge that
they would not be identified as unmarried mothers encouraged
women, for whom the loss of respectability would have been a
disaster, to entrust their children to the Hospital. Even the lights
in the entrance to the house were extinguished, so that the
women could not be identified as they approached, holding their
tiny bundles.

Many babies had to be turned away. In order to prevent their
disappointed parents from simply dumping them at the Hospital,
watchmen were hired to patrol the street and the porter was
instructed not to let any mothers leave until their children had
been formally admitted or else returned to them.

By midnight, the Hospital was full. It had received its first 18
boys and 12 girls. Two of this first intake died before they could be
baptised. The first two children to be baptised were named Thomas
Coram and Eunice Coram; others were named after the 'Persons
of Quality and Distinction' who had contributed to the Hospital.

About Twelve o'Clock, the House being full the Porter was Order'd to give Notice of it to the Crowd who were without, who thereupon being a little troublesom One of the Govrs. went out, and told them that as many Children were already taken in as Cou'd be made Room for in the House and that Notice Shou'd be given by a Publick Advertisement as soon as any more Could possibly be admitted. And the Govrs observing seven or eight women with Children at the Door and more amongst the Crowd desired them that they woul'd not Drop any of their Children in the Streets where they most probably must Perish but to take care of them till they could have an opportunity of putting them into the Hospital which was hoped would be very soon ... On this Occasion the Expressions of Grief of the Women whose Children could not be admitted were Scarcely more observable than those of some of the Women who parted with their Children, so that a more moving Scene can't well be imagined.'

(Foundling Hospital Daily Committee Minutes, 26 March 1741)

'There are at Paris, Madrid, Lisbon, Rome, and many other large Towns, great Hospitals built like our Colleges.'

(Addison, writing in the *Guardian*, 11 July 1713)

Building the Hospital

By the end of 1740, the Governors had found a site suitable for a purpose-built hospital. They paid the Earl of Salisbury £7,000 for 56 acres of his pasture land lying north of what is now Guilford Street and west of Gray's Inn Road. This site, well beyond the northern edge of the built-up part of Bloomsbury, offered space, quiet, fresh air and a view of green fields.

An architectural competition was announced for a hospital to house 400 children. The winning design was the one submitted by Theodore Jacobsen, an accomplished amateur architect who also happened to be one of the Governors. He envisaged a brick building with two residential wings and a central chapel, built around a courtyard that was open to the south. Arcaded walkways ran along the sides of the courtyard, providing an area for exercise in wet weather.

Jacobsen's design was frankly dull, but it was serviceable and its very plainness recommended it to the Governors, who were anxious not to be accused of spending charitable donations on fripperies for the Foundlings.

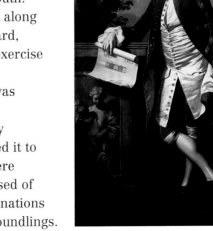

Thomas Hudson
(1701–79)
Theodore Jacobsen,
1742

John Rocque's map of London, 1746 (detail). The site chosen for the new hospital (circled) was beyond the northern edge of the built-up part of London

A Chinese porcelain punchbowl, c1780/90 Jingdezhen, Jiangxi province.
Painted in China with a view of the Foundling Hospital after a European print. The reverse shows a view of Vauxhall Gardens. (Donated in 2008 to the Foundling Museum by Catherine, Antonia and Lucy Newton in memory of their mother, Jan a foundling pupil).

Moreover, it could be built in stages, as funds permitted. The foundation stone of the west wing was laid in September 1742 and this first phase of the building was opened to the children within three years. The west wing eventually became the boys' quarters, with the Governors' Court Room and the Picture Gallery on the first floor. The east wing, where the girls lived, was built between 1749 and 1752. Each wing housed 192 children, sleeping two to a bed.

The interior of the children's accommodation was plain but clean and well lit. It had a logical layout that was easy for little children to understand, even if they were intimidated by the scale or the austerity of their new home. Elaborate architectural decoration was reserved for the Chapel and the Governors' offices—especially the Court Room, which was adorned with elegant plasterwork. Besides reinforcing the social distinction between the Foundlings and their guardians, this contrast reflected the twin functions of the building, which was not only a shelter for abandoned children but also a place where polite society and potential donors could be received and entertained.

Fundraising

The evident success and scale of the Hospital project attracted donations in cash and in kind. Jacobsen provided his architectural expertise free of charge, as did James Horne, the surveyor who supervised the building project. The magnificent rococo ceiling in the Court Room and the decorative plasterwork in the Chapel were by the plasterer William Wilton, who gave both the materials and his services for nothing. The Chapel, begun in May 1747,

John Sanders
(1750–1825)
The *Girls' Dining Room*, 1773.
This shows the girls wearing their neat, red-trimmed uniforms. Hogarth's portrait of Captain Coram hangs to the right of the fireplace

attracted a disproportionate number of gifts, no doubt because the donors realised that more people would see this part of the Hospital and because supporting a religious building had none of the potentially embarrassing connotations that might attach to funding the care of the children. The composer George Frideric Handel paid for the first organ in the Chapel, and the pulpit was designed and supplied, again for free, by the architect Henry Keene. Even the altar railings were donated by the smith who made them, Mr Wragg.

Although the Governors welcomed free goods and services, they needed to raise large amounts of cash for their ambitious building programme. The cost of building the east wing was largely paid for by Thomas Emerson, one of the Governors, and George II himself gave £2,000 towards the building of the Chapel, but the Hospital could not rely on such large donations occurring regularly. The Governors therefore embarked on an imaginative and innovative fundraising programme. Many of the methods of attracting donations that we now take for granted, such as charity balls, fundraising concerts or celebrities endorsing good causes, originated at the Foundling Hospital.

From the beginning, the Governors wanted the Hospital to be a place where the fashionable and wealthy might come to admire the buildings, inspect the children, view the art collection, attend services in the Chapel—and make handsome donations. Money was raised by the sale of tickets to Ladies' Breakfasts, at which women of fashion would be persuaded to make further donations. The social *cachet* of attending these events was enormous: at one Breakfast, held on 1 May 1747 to raise money for the Chapel building fund, the windows had to be nailed shut to prevent

Emma King, née Brownlow (1832–1905), *The Christening*, 1863. The newly-received Foundlings are being baptised, unusually, at the altar—a setting that allows the artist to depict the altar rails and, in the background, Benjamin West's painting, *Christ presenting a Little Child*, which replaced Andrea Casali's *The Adoration of the Magi* in 1801

uninvited guests from sneaking in. On another occasion, the High Constable and six assistants—bouncers, in effect—had to be hired to control the crowds.

Music in the Chapel

Concerts were another effective method of raising money for the building fund, and the Hospital became famous for performances organised and conducted by Handel. As a boy, Handel would have known of Professor Francke's famously progressive orphanage in his hometown, Halle in Saxony. The childless composer may have been moved by memories of this orphanage when he heard about the Foundling Hospital from the music publisher and Governor,

John Sanders (1750–1825), *Interior of Chapel, looking west*, 1773. The Sunday services attracted large congregations, drawn by the high standard of music. The organ shown in this view is the one given to the Hospital by Handel in 1750; it was replaced in 1775

Louis-François Roubiliac (1705–1762), *George Frideric Handel* (1685–1759). Roubiliac's portrait in terracotta is the model for a marble bust of Handel made in 1739 and now in the Royal Collection at Windsor Castle. It was presented to the Hospital by Sir Frederick Pollock in 1844. At the time of the donation, it was covered with plaster and paint 'and seemed to be no more than a second-rate object'. It was revealed as a masterpiece by the great baroque sculptor in 1966, following restoration by the Victoria and Albert Museum

John Walsh, in 1749. He may also have been inspired by the example set by another famous composer: in the 1730s, Antonio Vivaldi had attracted fashionable crowds to the *Pietà* orphanage in Venice, where he was concert master.

Handel 'Generously & Charitably offered a Performance of Vocal and Instrumental Musick' to raise funds for the completion of the Chapel. The offer was accepted and in May 1749 the composer conducted a benefit concert in the Chapel, with a programme that included the first performance of his *Foundling Hospital Anthem*.

The following year Handel conducted the first of his many performances of the *Messiah* in the Chapel, the concert opening on the organ he had just donated. The tickets for this event included a request that gentlemen would not wear swords nor ladies their hooped skirts, so as to make more room for the large audience that was anticipated. On the night of the concert, so many tickets had been sold on the door that advance subscribers were being turned away, so Handel undertook to repeat the performance a fortnight later. Shortly thereafter he agreed to become a Governor. *Messiah* became an annual event, Handel attending every performance until his death in 1759, even after illness prevented him from conducting. All the musical performances were well attended; one concert alone raised 500 guineas for the Hospital.

In his will, Handel bequeathed a fair copy of the *Messiah* to the Hospital. (illustrated p.82)

Art and philanthropy: Hogarth's contribution

The most remarkable contribution to the Foundling Hospital was made by William Hogarth and his friends from the St Martin's Lane Academy of Art, a group that included several of the leading British artists of the time. Hogarth has been described as 'the most energetic, controversial, and ultimately influential figure in the London arts scene of the 1740s'. He was also extremely ambitious. By the time his association with the Foundling Hospital began he was already a renowned painter of portraits, historical paintings and 'modern moral subjects' and was equally famous as an engraver. He had also begun to associate himself with good causes as a way of gaining a foothold in polite society and of creating opportunities to exhibit his work to potential patrons. He had become a Governor of St Bartholomew's Hospital in 1734, and had carried out two large paintings for the Staircase Hall of that hospital's new building, free of charge, in 1736–7. This very public support for Bart's helped him to secure several private commissions for portraits of eminent physicians practising in London in the 1730s and '40s.

The Foundling Hospital was another opportunity for self-promotion. Hogarth was involved with the Hospital from the very beginning, and was one of the first Governors to be appointed. There is evidence, however, that Hogarth's interest in the project was more than just a way to further his career. His outstanding contribution to the Foundling Hospital must have had a more personal motivation. Perhaps he found Coram a particularly sympathetic figure. The two men certainly had much in common: they both came from humble origins and had to make their own way in the world. Both were childless yet fond of children. Each in

William Hogarth (1697–1764), *Captain Thomas Coram***, 1740 (detail)**

John Michael Rysbrack (1694–1770) *Charity and Children engaged in Navigation and Husbandry*, 1745. This white marble relief was designed to fit the chimneypiece of the Court Room, and was presented to the Hospital by the artist. The figure of Charity suckles an infant in the shade of an oak tree in full leaf. At her feet, naked infants coil a rope next to an anchor (the symbol of hope). To the right, another figure milks a cow and two more *putti* cut and bind corn, anticipating the careers that await the foundling boys.

his own way fought for the rights of the underprivileged and exploited (while Coram was trudging round London collecting signatures for his petitions, Hogarth was almost single-handedly responsible for the passing of the Engravers' Copyright Act of 1735, which protected artists' rights to their own work). Both attacked hypocrisy and injustice in the social order, but whereas Coram tackled these with innocent directness, the more worldly Hogarth did so through sly and sophisticated images such as *The Harlot's Progress* or *Marriage à-la-Mode*.

In 1740, the painter presented his great portrait of Captain Coram to the Governors. This was long before the Hospital had any room to house it, but it was an indication of Hogarth's ambition to form an important art collection at the Hospital. As the self-appointed champion of British art, Hogarth wanted to promote a native school of art that would equal any in Europe. He could assemble such a school from among his own friends who were painters and sculptors, but there were no public galleries or museums in London where they could display their work. Hogarth saw that the new Hospital could be the perfect solution to this problem. His inspired idea was to persuade the artists to donate paintings and sculptures to the Hospital. The scheme gave the artists the chance not only to cement their social position through well-publicised acts of charity, but also to ensure that their work would be seen by the public, and in particular by the aristocratic and wealthy patrons of the Hospital—exactly the sort of people who might commission works of art for themselves.

In December 1746, several artists offered 'to present Performances in their different Professions for Ornamenting the

Hospital'. The Governors could not spend the Hospital's funds on mere embellishments, so all the works of art were donated by the artists. In return, the artists were elected Governors and formed a separate committee 'to meet Annually on the 5th of November to consider of what further Ornaments may be added to this Hospital without any expence to the Charity.' The names of the artists' committee form a roll-call of the most distinguished artists practising in London: besides Hogarth and his fellow founder-Governor, the sculptor John Michael Rysbrack, they include the painters Francis Hayman, Joseph Highmore, Thomas Hudson, George Moser, John Pine, Allan Ramsay, Samuel Scott, Samuel Wale, James Wills and Richard Wilson. Thomas Gainsborough and Joshua Reynolds also contributed works, although they were not members of the committee.

History painting—including biblical subjects—was considered the loftiest branch of art, and so it was a series of large-scale paintings of religious scenes that was unveiled in the Court Room on 1 April 1747, at a public dinner hosted by the Governors. This was the nucleus of what was to become an outstanding collection of eighteenth-century art, which survives intact as 'a unique experiment in the education of public taste'. The dinner was the first step towards turning the Foundling Hospital into an arts centre or entertainment complex, where pictures could be viewed, concerts enjoyed, church services attended, and public acts of charity admired, all in the warm glow of philanthropic goodwill.

The paintings attracted flocks of visitors, proving that there was a demand for public exhibitions of paintings by living British artists. With this encouragement, the artist-Governors began to look for other opportunities for exhibiting their work in London.

After Samuel Wale (1721–86), *Admission of Children to the Hospital by Ballot*. Engraving by N. Parr, published 9 May 1749. The silk gowns of the ladies of fashion who have come to observe the spectacle of the ballot are poignantly contrasted with the simple cloaks and aprons of the mothers who are hoping to find a safe home for their babies

In time, their regular meetings led to the founding of the Royal Academy of Arts, which has continued the tradition of an annual public exhibition in London since 1768.

Coram's Children: The luck of the draw

On the days appointed for receiving children, crowds of women with their babies would gather at the entrance to the Hospital. The Governors might accept 20 infants at a time but there were often up to 100 awaiting admission, and it was not surprising that there were 'disorderly scenes' as desperate mothers fought one another for a place at the front of the crowd. The Governors decided that a ballot would be a fairer method of allocating places. Hopeful mothers attended 'reception' days when, in front of an audience of the wealthy and respectable, they were each invited to draw one ball out of a bag: the colour of the ball—white, black or red—would decide the fate of the child. A white ball meant the baby would be examined and admitted if it was healthy. A black ball, and the mother was 'immediately turned out of the Hospital with her child'. Mothers who drew a red ball could wait to see whether any babies were refused admittance, in which case they would be given a second chance to enter this agonising lottery.

A token of devotion

No questions were asked of a mother who brought her child to the Hospital, apart from what parish she came from and whether the baby had been baptised. However, a careful record of each child was made, noting appearance, distinguishing marks, clothes and any other identifying information. Mothers pinned notes and keepsakes to their baby's clothes, and these tokens—a coin, a

ring, a scrap of ribbon, a button, or even the label from a beer bottle—are among the most touching items in the Hospital's collection. In return the mother received a document that certified the Hospital's acceptance of her baby. An admittance number that corresponded to the written record was stamped on a lead tag attached to a necklace; this was placed around the child's neck, and the nurses and other employees of the Hospital were forbidden to remove it.

The paperwork was useful in two important respects. Throughout the Hospital's history, parents applied to reclaim children they had reluctantly surrendered. The records enabled the Governors to be sure that it they were restoring the right child to its family. Having convinced the Governors of their reformed character and improved circumstances, parents were usually required to pay for the child's care. The demand for payment was discontinued in 1764 and thereafter, three or four children were reunited each year with their parents. The second, rather more

London Foundling Hospital, girls exercising. Outdoor exercise was advocated for the children from the earliest years

disturbing, use of the Hospital's records was in the defence of mothers who were accused of having disposed of their babies by murdering them. If they could produce certificates that matched the Hospital's records of adoption, they might save themselves from the gallows.

Overwhelming demand

Of the 2,523 children who sought places between January 1750 and December 1755, only 783 were admitted. The Hospital simply did not have the funds to house more, but its very existence, by attracting such large numbers of desperate parents to beg for a place for their children, drew attention to the need for better provision. In 1756, the Governors petitioned Parliament for more funds and were eventually allocated a grant of £10,000, on condition that all children presented for admission were accepted. The Governors immediately ordered more furniture and bedding, recruited more staff (including nurses from as far afield as Yorkshire), and announced a General Reception between June and December 1756. In the first two weeks, 299 children arrived and the Hospital administration was nearly overwhelmed by the task of finding nurses and allocating places to all the infants.

The General Reception was a shameless attempt by the Government to make a single private charity solve the embarrassing national problem of abandoned infants and it was a disaster. Poor Law officers saw an opportunity to unburden their parishes of responsibility for foundlings, and started sending tightly swaddled babies to Bloomsbury by pack horse. Many did not survive the journey. Distressed mothers in rural areas might pay to have a child taken to London, but unscrupulous traffickers

Detail from Coram's Children exhibition of the list of names of children admitted into the Foundling Hospital between 1741–56. Throughout the Hospital's history foundlings were baptised with a new name on entry. These names represent the generations who passed through the Hospital

were as likely to abandon the baby to die *en route* as to deposit it safely at the Hospital. Six subsidiary hospitals were hastily set up, at Ackworth, Aylesbury, Barnet, Chester, Shrewsbury and Westerham, but could not cope with the demand. Many infants were in poor health on admission and mortality rates leapt from the previous rate of around 30%, which was considered acceptable, to 70%, which was not. Public opinion began to turn against the Hospital. Further grants from Parliament were not enough to ease the financial pressure and the General Reception ended in 1760 after the admission of almost 15,000 children.

A period of recovery followed: except for a handful of children orphaned when their soldier fathers were killed on active service, the Hospital admitted no Foundlings between March 1760 and 1763. However, it is to the Hospital's credit that it cared for all the children received during the General Reception until they were at least 21 and in the case of disabled children, remained their guardian for life.

From 1763 the ballot was suspended and mothers were instead required to state their name and explain why they could not care for their children. Although it was not until 1795 that the Hospital formally acknowledged its secondary purpose as the 'restoration of the mother to work and a life of virtue', a destitute unmarried woman knew she had to establish her good character before she could expect any help. Most petitions pleading for a child's admission came from women who claimed to have been seduced with promises of marriage only to be deserted when they became pregnant, but there are also accounts of rape. Many mothers argued that they could only avoid disgrace and find employment if they did not have to care for their children. Some

of the petitions are from illiterate servant girls who asked better-educated friends to write on their behalf and endorsed the documents with crude signatures or scrawled crosses. Nearly all the petitions reveal the anguish and distress mothers suffered at having to give up their beloved children.

In 1768, the Governors decided that admission was to be at the discretion of the General Committee. Petitioning continued but balloting was also used when candidates exceeded the number of available places. From 1801, the Hospital's 'principal object' became the maintenance and support of illegitimate children. Illegitimacy became a requirement for admission, with occasional exceptions for the orphans of soldiers and sailors.

Out to nurse

Once accepted, babies did not usually stay in the Hospital but were placed with wet nurses as soon as possible, to be fostered until they were old enough to be returned to the Hospital, at between three and six years old. Nurses often lived in nearby country districts and were the wives of agricultural workers and artisans. A medical examination verified their good health and they received a monthly wage and a 10-shilling bonus if the children survived a year in their care. They were supervised by voluntary local Inspectors (Hogarth served as Inspector for Chiswick), who were responsible for nurses' pay and medical fees and for purchasing clothes for the infants. It was sometimes difficult to recruit Inspectors. One local organiser 'in vain endeavoured to get several Gentlemen in the Neighbourhood to assist her ... but all refused saying they would not be troubled about Bastards.' On the whole, however, the system worked well and the Foundlings were reasonably well looked after.

The children naturally regarded these nurses as their mothers and the nurses' attachment to the Foundlings was also strong. One commentator noted that 'the nurse showed the most lively sorrow in parting with them'. Some nurses even 'adopted' their charges by apprenticing them to their husbands at an unusually young age, perhaps six or seven. Alternatively, the child might return to the nurse's family after leaving the Hospital, apprenticed in the usual way.

Many Foundlings described this early period of their lives as happy, although there were cases of cruel and abusive nurses throughout the Hospital's history.

'A child of this Hospital'

Removal from the foster family must have been traumatic. Having previously lived as one of the family in a country labourer's cottage, the child was suddenly thrust into the very different environment of the Hospital, following a strict routine under close supervision alongside large numbers of other children. He or she soon discovered that every aspect of life within the Hospital—clothing, diet, education, exercise and even treats and entertainments—was matched to the Foundlings' actual and anticipated station in life. Foundlings were expected to be honest, humble, grateful, hardworking and obedient to their superiors. Religious education was emphasised and continued even into apprenticeship. The Hospital routine was designed to ensure that the Foundlings became dutiful and productive servants, artisans and soldiers.

The staff seem to have been correct rather than affectionate in

Harold Copping *A Foundling Boy* and *A Foundling Girl*, both 1919. These portraits show how little the Foundlings' uniforms had changed since Hogarth's day. The children are dressed for the careers that have been chosen for them: domestic service for the girl, military service for the boy

their attitude towards the children, who consequently found it difficult to form close relationships, even with other Foundlings. Petty bullying was endemic, and since every child experienced the same dull routines, wore the same clothes and ate the same food as every other child in the Hospital, it hardly mattered who they played with or talked to—every friendship was the same. Customs and slang handed down from one generation of Foundlings to the next gave a sense of belonging that was a poor substitute for the affectionate intimacy of family life; women were referred to, heartbreakingly, as 'mums'.

Clothes

On entering the Hospital, the children had their hair cut and were issued with a uniform. The earliest design for the Foundlings' uniform has been attributed to Hogarth and dates from 1745–6. The clothes were made and repaired by the older children in their sewing lessons and were constructed from sturdy materials so as to be cheap, hard-wearing and long-lasting.

The boys wore white linen shirts with breeches and jackets made of brown Yorkshire serge and trimmed with red. The girls had white linen shifts over which they wore dresses of the same brown serge with red edging. Over this, they wore a bib and apron of unbleached linen. The girls' uniforms resembled those of domestic servants. The boys' uniforms were smarter and military in style. Both indicated the Foundlings' probable future occupations.

Each May, the children received new sets of clothes, including enough 'body linen' to ensure that they could always be clean and neat. Both sexes were given coats made of heavy wool cloth and

They rise at six in the summer and daylight in winter, part of them being employed before breakfast in dressing the younger children, in cleaning about the house, and the boys in working a forcing pump which supplies all the wards and every part of the Hospital abundantly with water. At half past seven they breakfast and at half after eight into school, where they continue, the boys till twelve, the girls a little later. At one o'clock they dine, and return to school at two, and stay till four in the summer, and in winter till dusk, except on Saturday when they have half-holiday. They are also instructed in singing the Foundling Hymns and anthems, and in their catechism, and are occasionally employed in and about the house during play-hours. At six in the evening they sup, and at eight go to bed.

(The daily routine of the Hospital at the turn of the eighteenth century, described by Sir Thomas Bernard, Treasurer)

Engraving by J. Swain after H.T. Thomas This image from the *Illustrated London News*, 7 December 1872 shows wealthy families visiting the Foundling Hospital on a Sunday, to watch the children enjoying their lunch and to view the works of art lining the walls, which remained a fashionable pursuit

were issued with shoes and stockings—important indicators of respectability. When they left the Hospital to take up apprenticeships, the Foundlings took with them a complete set of clothes, but even these were merely a variation on the familiar brown-and-red livery.

Long years spent in uniform may have reinforced the children's sense of their low status and denied them individuality, but at the very least, they were warmly and respectably attired, and began life with better wardrobes than many of their contemporaries.

Food

All the children in the Hospital received the same simple diet, repeated weekly and consisting of a light breakfast, a heavier midday meal and a light supper. Bread appeared at nearly every meal and meat was served at least three times a week. Sloppy, filling dishes such as gruel, rice pudding, broth and porridge all appear regularly in the Hospital's Tables of Diet. Fruit and vegetables were occasionally eaten. The Hospital had its own garden, and the records mention fruit trees and a melon patch, so presumably the children ate the seasonal produce, although as this did not have to be paid for, it does not show up in the accounts.

The children were not given any fish, eggs, poultry, tea or beer. The omission of beer was unusual, as in the eighteenth century it was regarded as a food and was a safer drink than water drawn from wells and pumps, which were often contaminated. Sweets or puddings only appeared on special occasions.

The emphasis on bread and meat would not be regarded as particularly healthy today and the amounts of fruit, vegetables and calcium were wholly inadequate—but by eighteenth-century

**Allan Ramsay
(1713–84),
Dr Richard Mead, 1747**

standards the children were eating a diet of plain, wholesome
food in reasonable quantity. Checks were made to ensure that the
food was fresh and of good quality, that the milk was not watered
down nor the flour adulterated with alum. From time to time the
Governors sampled the cooking themselves: in 1790 one of them
complained that the beef broth was 'as salt as brine' and
described a pudding as 'extremely bad, consisting of milk & flour
& sugar boiled only to the consistency of thick paste'.

Food accounted for a large proportion of the Hospital's budget.
But even when costs rose and the Hospital became financially
constrained, the Governors did not compromise the children's
diet. It is likely that the portions were small, as many Foundlings
complained of constant hunger. However, compared with poor
children living with their families, the Foundlings had a
reasonable diet.

Health

From the outset, the Governors were concerned with the
children's health. Good health was an important admission
criterion, and babies who had symptoms of infectious disease—
'French Pox, Evil, Leprosy, or Disease of the Like Nature'—were
turned away. Breast-feeding by wet nurses, and loose clothing
instead of restrictive swaddling were recommended for infants.
These were advanced ideas at the time.

The Hospital promoted good health through preventive
measures such as separating the sick from the well, keeping
rooms well aired, general cleanliness, outdoor exercise,
immersion in cold baths and the destruction of any contaminated
clothing. These progressive measures were influenced by

Emma King, née Brownlow (1832–1905), *The Sick Room*, 1864. This view of the conditions in which sick Foundlings were nursed is possibly somewhat idealised

Governors such as Dr William Cadogan, Dr Richard Mead and Sir Hans Sloane. Throughout its history the Hospital had access to the first rank of medical expertise. Dr Robert Nesbitt, Sir William Watson and Dr John Mayo all attended subsequent generations of children without charge. The Hospital was also advanced in having its own apothecary and its own dedicated infirmary on a separate site. Few children, whether from rich or poor families, received medical care of the standard provided by the Hospital.

Even so, there were regular epidemics of the serious illnesses that used to be regarded as an inevitable feature of childhood, such as measles (one of the most frequent causes of death) and whooping cough. In 1763 an epidemic of scarlet fever infected more than 150 children and caused nine deaths. However, the chief scourge of childhood was smallpox, which was frequently fatal, sometimes caused blindness and nearly always disfigured the faces of its victims. The Hospital was very advanced in its approach to this disease: as early as 1744 children were routinely inoculated against smallpox.

Less dramatically, the Governors and senior staff waged a constant battle with the domestic staff to ensure decent standards of cleanliness. So many children living at close quarters were irresistibly attractive to bedbugs, lice and nits. If an outbreak of 'the itch' (scabies—a highly infectious rash) took hold, It could take months to eradicate it.

Developmental defects due to malnutrition were common. Lack of fresh fruit and vegetables in the children's diet caused scurvy (indicating a deficiency of vitamin C) rickets (vitamin D) and poor eyesight (vitamin A), and a general lack of protein meant that most Foundlings grew up to be noticeably shorter than average.

Notwithstanding the innocence of the Children, yet as they are exposed and abandoned by their Parents, they ought to submit to the lowest stations and should not be educated in such a manner as may put them upon a level with the Children of Parents who have the Humanity and Virtue to preserve them, and the Industry to Support them.

(Foundling Hospital sub-committee minutes, 12 April 1749)

Education

Seeking to save lives *and* turn children into useful citizens, the Hospital emphasised Christian duty and provided an education suitable for the Foundlings' future working lives. Eventually, it was assumed, the boys would join the army or navy or be apprenticed and the girls would enter domestic service.

Aware of possible objections to their creating a well-educated workforce who could compete on equal terms with the children of respectable families, the Governors proclaimed their intention of training the Foundlings 'to undergo with Contentment the most Servile and laborious Offices'. In the Hospital's early years, therefore, children received a very limited education. Basic literacy was all they would require in their working lives, it was argued, and to give them more was not only redundant but might give them ideas above their station.

Between the ages of three and six the children were taught to read, so that they could study the Bible. Indeed, no other reading matter was provided, apart from the Hospital's 'Instructions to Apprentices'. Writing was not taught, as it would not be required in employment. Teaching, meanwhile, was regarded as a humble occupation, requiring no special skills.

In 1757 the Hospital employed its first professional teachers. A schoolmistress taught the girls—in classes of 50 at a time and with the emphasis not on reading (and certainly not writing or mathematics) but on spinning, knitting, needlework, prayers and the catechism of the Church of England. The first schoolmaster, Mr Redpath, was an innovator who ordered new sheets of alphabets and basic reading books, and introduced a new timetable for the boys by which they spent half the day working

London Foundling Hospital, girls' schoolroom, early 20th century

and half at lessons. Even playtime was turned to good use: play was for forming healthy bodies, and so boys were drilled in military marching, and girls were made to walk upright 'without wadling'.

The Governors' attitude to education changed gradually, along with that of society as a whole, so that by 1800 all the boys were being taught to read and write and some were learning arithmetic, while all the girls were being taught to read, and some to write and even do basic bookkeeping, alongside the housekeeping skills designed to fit them for domestic service. By the mid-nineteenth century both boys and girls were taught reading, writing, maths, English grammar and geography, as well as their catechism. Later in the Hospital's history, some children won academic distinction in later life but for most education remained rudimentary.

Educational methods within the Hospital emphasised reward rather than punishment. A child who did well at gardening, knitting, sewing, reading or writing might receive a small and appropriate present, such as a silver thimble, a pair of scissors, gingerbread, or even 'a Bible & Prayer Book, better bound than common, with initial Letter of the Boys & Girls Names in Gold Letters'. The gifts were to encourage the children 'thereby to Industry thro' the most powerful motive of self Interest' and 'to cause emulation in others'. Although the children were beaten to punish them for mischief, the beatings had to be authorised and supervised by the Matron and were never severe. For a time in the 1770s persistently naughty children were shut in a dark cupboard and kept on bread and water until they apologised— which might now be considered an equally severe form of discipline.

Be not ashamed that you were bred in this Hospital. Own it; and say that it was thro' the good Providence of Almighty God that you were taken care of. Bless Him for it; and be thankful to those worthy Benefactors who have contributed towards your Maintenance & Support. And if ever it be in your Power, make a grateful Acknowledgement to the Hospital for the Benefits you have received.

(From the Foundling Hospital's 'Instructions to Apprentices')

One striking aspect of a Hospital education, perhaps due to Handel's influence, was that the children were taught music. They were trained in choral singing and those with the best voices sang in the Chapel choir. Ensuring a high standard of music at Sunday services was important, as it drew large congregations whose contributions to the collections were a significant source of income for the Hospital. The more musical children were taught to play instruments, and several blind children were trained to a professional standard so that they could earn their living from playing and singing. Many of the boys later joined military bands.

Apprenticeship

The problem of what to do with the children once they reached the age of ten was solved by finding apprenticeships for them. The Governors took a great deal of care to find suitable employment for their charges. Prospective employers were visited and inspected, and their background and finances verified so that the Governors could be sure that they were entrusting the children to respectable people who could teach a trade and properly house, feed and clothe an apprentice.

The Contract signed by the master stipulated that he would provide 'sufficient Meat, Drink and Apparel, Lodging, Washing and all other things necessary & fit for an Apprentice.' Masters also undertook to ensure that their apprentices said their prayers night and morning and attended church every Sunday. For their part, the children were issued with a set of 'Instructions to Apprentices' that governed their behaviour. As well as a set of clothes, they were given copies of the Bible and the Book of Common Prayer when they left the Hospital.

Nearly all the girls became domestic servants, while the list of trades taken up by boys who did not go into the Army or Navy included cobbler, butcher, blacksmith, silk dyer, weaver and calico printer. After an apprenticeship of at least seven years (some lasted until the apprentice was 24), they were fully qualified to earn their living as journeymen, plying their trade for a daily rate.

The Governors followed the apprentices' progress, and would rescue them from unsatisfactory situations or prosecute where there was evidence of ill-treatment. But abuse could not always be avoided. In one instance, 22 of 74 apprentices sent to a Yorkshire wool manufacturer died within two years. Inspection revealed appalling living conditions, and the survivors were immediately moved elsewhere. There were one or two other cases of horrifying abuse that led to the death of the apprentice but the evidence suggests that most apprenticeships were successful. Few former Foundlings rose to great eminence but most were enabled to make a respectable living.

New approaches

Jacobsen's building served the Foundling Hospital well for 180 years but in 1926 the decision was taken to move the Hospital out of London. The Bloomsbury site was sold and the Hospital was demolished, apart from a few fragments. The Governors felt it was important to have an office in central London and wished to maintain their historic connection with Bloomsbury, so they repurchased a plot near the north-west corner of the Hospital site and commissioned a new headquarters building from the architect John Sheppard. His neo-Georgian design for 40 Brunswick Square, into which several of the historic interiors

Boys marching out of the London Foundling Hospital for the last time in 1926 before the building was demolished and the children relocated, first to Redhill and in 1936 to the new Hospital at Berkhamsted

from Jacobsen's building were incorporated, was completed in 1938. Six of the acres that had been sold were later bought back following a fundraising appeal and reopened to the public as Coram's Fields, a childrens' playground. Today (2009) it is run by an independent charity, The Harmsworth Trust.

The Governors later opened a nursery, nursery school and welfare centre on the northern part of the site.

Sheppard also designed a new set of buildings, closely modelled on Jacobsen's layout, for the new Hospital site at Berkhamsted in Hertfordshire. The education the children received was improved and broadened so that, although most of the girls were still being trained for domestic service, the brighter ones could go on to higher education. Most of the boys continued to join the Army, many of them as musicians in Army bands. During the Second World War the Hospital housed 680 pupils, the largest number since the eighteenth century.

In the late 1940s and early 1950s, there were gradual changes in the way the children's care was managed. Mothers were encouraged to remain in contact with their children, long-term fostering became the norm and fewer children were accepted— which meant that those who did 'live in' could receive more individual attention. Even so, the regime was strict, as one former Foundling, interviewed in the late 1990s, recalled: 'It was military

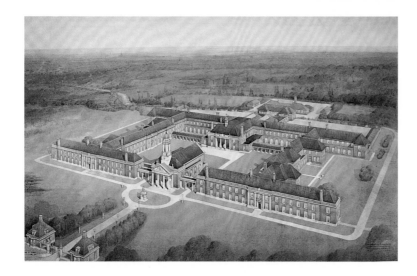

Cyril Farey
(1888–1954)
*The Foundling
Hospital School,
Berkhamsted,
Hertfordshire.*
On ceasing to be the
Foundling Hospital the
school passed to the
local authority and
runs today (2009) as
Ashlyn's School

style. It was "here is a job I've got to do, get on with it." ... so the
staff were not unkind, but certainly not loving. They didn't want to
know if you had a problem really. They'd got a job to do. You had
to follow and obey orders what they said and if you didn't, you
were in trouble. It was a monastic sort of existence. As long as
you kept going, you were okay.'

New social attitudes and approaches to child care were
reflected in changes in the administration of the Hospital. By 1953
the old institutional model of care was outdated, and the Hospital
adopted a policy of placing all its children in foster homes. The
charity was renamed the Thomas Coram Foundation for Children,
a change that honoured the founder and implied a less impersonal
attitude toward the families it served. The nursery and welfare
centre were redeveloped and opened in 1974 as the Coram
Children's Centre, which pioneered an integrated approach to the
care and education of children, co-ordinating the efforts of
everyone—parents, teachers, social and health workers—involved.

After further reorganisation the Foundation emerged in 1999
with a new name, Coram Family. Today the charity is now known
simply as 'Coram', it carries out a range of programmes, including
finding adoptive families for children with special needs and
specialist foster homes for very troubled and troublesome children
who would otherwise be sent to secure accommodation, providing
a contact service so that children can stay in touch with their
parents, and supporting young people as they prepare to leave the
care system and lead independent lives.

The Foundling Hospital's large collection of paintings,
sculpture, furniture, clocks and historical documents came under
the care of a separate museum trust in 1998.

The Foundling Museum
– a tour

The exterior of 40 Brunswick Square is of the London stock brick typical of Bloomsbury townhouses. Its classical plainness is embellished only by a carved stone head of Thomas Coram and two roundels of children, above the front door. The interior incorporates some key elements from Jacobsen's Hospital: the Court Room, the Committee Room, the Picture Gallery and the oak staircase from the west wing were all recreated within the shell of the new building using the original materials, which had been carefully dismantled in 1926 and stored with a view to re-erection in the new premises.

In 2004, following an extensive renovation and rebuilding programme, No. 40 reopened as the Foundling Museum. It houses the works of art that were given to the Foundling Hospital, along with documents and artefacts recording the history of the institution. Together, these form a unique and poignant record of a pioneering philanthropic enterprise.

Ground floor

From the entrance hall and ticket office, turn right into the exhibition *Coram's Children*, which explains the origins and history of the Foundling Hospital. The exhibition combines materials from the Museum and archive collections to reflect social conditions in eighteenth-century London and the lives of children in the care of the Foundling Hospital.

In one of the cases is the Headpiece for the subscription roll for the Foundling Hospital dated 1739. Designed by William Hogarth, it depicts Captain Coram holding the Hospital Charter and

overleaf: General view of Coram's Children exhibition with a specially commissioned film 'Roots and Wings', written and directed by Jonathan Hourigan, produced by Jason Underhill

Children

Every child and every generation of children, throughout history and across the globe, **represents the future.**

In many cultures the child is revered. Just as the elderly person or the mother is revered in other cultures.

But the child, naturally trusting and full of love, is also uniquely vulnerable.

Vulnerable to active, wilful cruelty and abuse by individuals. But also vulnerable to the passive neglect of individuals, or entire societies, that do not love, cherish, protect and nurture their children, who are their future.

We were our parents' future.

Today, our children, across the globe, are our future.

They are our individual and collective responsibilities. And none more so than the vulnerable, the abandoned, the sick, the hungry and the unloved.

The courageous, shining example of Captain Coram continues to illuminate the way forward, perhaps today more than ever before.

George Frideric Handel, *The Foundling Hospital Anthem*, 1749

The *Foundling Hospital Anthem* is a setting of a text adapted from Psalm 41 beginning 'Blessed are They that Considereth the Poor'. Handel composed it especially for a concert of his music, held in May 1749 to raise funds for the Chapel. This copy of the score contains amendments in the composer's own handwriting

rescuing a baby from a desperate mother who is about to murder it. Another baby lies abandoned by a stream and a third is being left under a hedge. The Hospital, representing order and security, is surrounded by neatly-dressed children who carry the emblems of their intended trades. The Hospital is providing true Christian charity while the old institutions of church and parish remain—literally and metaphorically in the background.

Foundling tokens

Perhaps the most eloquent items in the Foundling Hospital collection are the objects left by mothers with their children as a unique means of identification, in case they were ever in a position to reclaim them. The tokens varied widely: metal tags engraved with the child's name and date of birth, ribbons, buttons, coins, lockets, base metal rings, elaborate brooches, rings and a hazel-nut shell. There were also written tokens and poems.

> Hard is my Lot in deep Distress
> To have no help where Most should find
> Sure Nature meant her sacred Laws
> Should men as strong as Women bind
> Regardless he, Unable I,
> To keep this Image of my Heart
> 'Tis vile to Murder! hard to Starve
> And Death almost to me to part
> If Fortune should her favours give
> That I in Better plight may Live
> I'd try to have my boy again
> And Train him up the best of Men.

The Committee Room

This room is one of the interiors from the original Foundling Hospital which were accurately reconstructed in the new headquarters. Within these walls, mothers came to be interviewed about the suitability of their children for adoption before they submitted to the ballot process. The contents of this room illustrate different aspects of childhood and the management of the Hospital in the eighteenth and nineteenth centuries.

Most of the pictures are scenes from childhood or incidents in the lives of the Foundlings. They are hung in the traditional manner from brass picture rods. The furniture includes a seventeenth-century elm refectory table, which was in everyday use in the Hospital during the eighteenth century. The Museum's collection of eighteenth-century communion silver, consisting of donated and specially-commissioned pieces, is a reminder of the importance of the Anglican religion in the day-to-day life and education of the children.

George Lambert (1700–65)
Landscape with Figures, 1757

Lambert collaborated with Hogarth on several projects, including the murals at St Bartholomew's Hospital and was one of the first artist-Governors of the Hospital. The artists were elected Governors on the understanding that each would give a painting to the Hospital: Lambert's gift, framed within the panelling on the chimneybreast, is an idealised vision of rural family life in a woodland setting. The chimneypiece and overmantel are said to have been designed by Hogarth.

overleaf: Hanslip
Fletcher
The Committee Room,
1925

William Hogarth (1697–1764)
The March of the Guards to Finchley, **painted 1749–50**
This 'view of a military march, and the humours and disorders
consequent thereupon' depicts a moment during the Jacobite
Rebellion of 1745, when a regiment of Guards, mustering in
Tottenham Court road, marched north out of London to meet the
Young Pretender's forces. Subscribers to the copperplate
engraving of the painting could pay an extra 3 shillings for a
lottery ticket that gave them a chance to win the original
painting—a common method of promoting artists' work in the
eighteenth century. Hogarth gave all the unsold tickets to the
Hospital and—to no-one's surprise—one of these bore the winning
number. 'The same Night,' reported the *London Evening Post*, 'Mr
Hogarth deliver'd the Picture to the Governors. His Grace the
Duke of Ancaster offer'd them £200 for it before it was taken
away, but it was refus'd.'

Staircase Hall

The oak staircase is the original staircase from the west wing of Jacobsen's building—minus the spiked iron rail added above the handrail in the eighteenth century to stop the boys sliding down it after one child who did so fell and was killed. The design of this staircase, with its bulbous, turned balusters and low, wide handrail, suggests the plain, utilitarian nature of the fittings in the Foundlings' accommodation.

The staircase walls are hung with portraits of Governors and paintings of religious subjects.

Lower Ground floor
Exhibitions

The Lower Ground floor contains the Exhibition Gallery which houses innovative temporary exhibitions throughout the year. Please consult our website, www.foundlingmuseum.org.uk or telephone the main reception, 020 7841 3600, for further details.

The Lower Ground floor also contains facilities for educational visits in a purpose-built education centre. For more information on educational programmes, visits for schools and special interest groups please contact the Learning Department on 020 7841 3605.

View of staircase with the sculpture of *Peasant Boy* (British School). The paintings are William Carter (1863–1939) *Mrs Patrick Forbes* and *Pinch of Poverty* by Thomas Kennington (1856–1915)

First floor
Landing

Andrea Casali (1720–83)
Adoration of the Magi, **completed 1750**
Casali's painting was originally (in 1752) installed above the altar
in the Chapel. In 1801 it was moved to the Boys' Dining Room in
the west wing of Jacobsen's building and its place in the Chapel
was taken by Benjamin West's *Christ presenting a Little Child*,
now displayed on the adjacent staircase.

Other objects on the landing associated with the Chapel are two
lead cartouches with appropriate Biblical quotations, presented by
the artist Edward Ives and a portable font made by the famous
firm of Coade & Sealy in 1804. The longcase clock, the finest in
the Hospital's collection, was presented by its maker, John Elliott
FRS in 1750

The Picture Gallery
This room is a replica of the Picture Gallery in the west wing of
Jacobsen's building. This was one of the principal attractions of
the Foundling Hospital, a permanent exhibition space where
polite society could enjoy the work of some of the best artists then
working in London.

The room is now devoted to large-scale portraits of Governors
and other figures associated with the Hospital. The drum table
dates from the reign of George IV.

overleaf: Picture
Gallery, 1930s replica
of the original
eighteenth-century
room

William Hogarth (1697–1764)
Captain Thomas Coram, 1740

In Hogarth's wonderful portrait, the founder of the Hospital is depicted with full baroque splendour: the classical column, tumbling drapery and panoply of attributes alluding to his life and achievements, are all in the grand manner. Yet the old man at the centre of all this pomp is portrayed with directness, sympathy and informality. His clothes are unpretentious and he is not wearing a wig. He sits upright, grasping the seal of the Royal Charter in one hand and his glove in the other, with a rather pugnacious expression on his face, as if ready to leap to the defence of his beloved Hospital.

Captain Coram can be compared with his near neighbours in the Picture Gallery, Ramsay's *Dr Richard Mead* (see page 64) and Hudson's *Theodore Jacobsen* (see page 65). Coram's tumbling white hair is an unruly halo compared with the tightly-curled wig of the doctor, and his dark suit and heavy coat are serviceable in contrast with the architect's sumptuous satin and velvet. Coram is alert and his pose suggests readiness for action, while Mead is statuesque and Jacobsen debonair. The portraits underline the differences in background and outlook between the founder of the Hospital and the men who made his scheme a practical reality and who would eventually exclude him from the Board of Governors.

Thomas Hudson (1701-79)
Portrait of John Milner (c1747)

John Milner, a barrister, was one of the Foundling Hospital's first vice-presidents. On 16th September 1742 he laid the Hospital's foundation stone. When demand for admission exceeded places he devised and oversaw the Hospital's ballot system. His correspondence with Dr Hans Soane helped set up the Hospital's enlightened regime in the rearing and nutrition of its infants. Milner was one of Thomas Coram's six pall-bearers "clad in deep mourning" at the founder's funeral on 3rd April 1751.

Allan Ramsay (1713–84)
Dr Richard Mead, 1747
Besides being one of the foremost physicians of his day, Mead had
an international reputation as a scholar, collector and antiquarian.
His medical background and professional connections made him
an ideal founding Governor of the Hospital.

Thomas Hudson (1701–79)
Theodore Jacobsen, 1742

Jacobsen was the architect of the Foundling Hospital and a
founding Governor. He is shown holding an engraving of the
Hospital and leaning on a plinth carved with a figure of Charity
with two infants.

Anteroom

The anteroom is dedicated to works on paper, including a series of pen and ink drawings by Hanslip Fletcher, recording the principal interiors of the Hospital in the mid-1920s, before it was demolished. There are also two important watercolour views of the the Girls' Dining Room and the Chapel, painted by John Sanders in 1773 (see pages 19 and 20).

Foyer

The paintings in this room illustrate nautical themes relating to the Hospital's connections with the sea. Many Foundlings were sent into the Navy when they were old enough to leave the Hospital.

John Singleton Copley (1738–1815)
The Siege and Relief of Gibraltar
This monochrome sketch was presented to the Hospital by Sir
Roger Gregory in 1925. It is a preparatory sketch for a painting in
the Guildhall Art Gallery, showing the British defeating the
Spanish navy off Gibraltar on 14 September 1782. General Elliot,
on a white horse, gestures towards British seamen rescuing the
enemy from their sinking ships.

The Court Room

The Court Room was the most important secular space in the Hospital. It was where the Board of Governors met, and where the most important functions for invited guests, such as the 'unveiling' dinner of 1747, were held. Its elaborate decoration reflected its high status and provided a impressive showcase for the talents of Hogarth and his brother artists.

The interior was carefully reconstructed in 1937. Only the 1930s veneered and inlaid floor (and carpet) did not come from Jacobsen's building. The glory of the architectural decoration is the rococo ceiling, a generous gift (and a spectacular self-advertisement) from the plasterer, William Wilton. The chandelier is a nineteenth-century reproduction of a conventional eighteenth-century design. The marble chimneypiece was carved by the Hospital's mason John Devall and donated in 1747. Devall also supplied the carved surround for the marble relief of *Charity* by Rysbrack, the second major work of art to be given to the Hospital (after Hogarth's portrait of Coram). The side table with a rectangular green marble top supported by carved figures of a goat and two children is another early gift, donated by the architect John Sanderson in 1745. The plaster busts of Caracalla and Marcus Aurelius are the only survivors of a set of 13 casts from the antique presented by Richard Dalton in 1753.

Archive photograph from the original Foundling Hospital of the Court Room, showing the fireplace with relief of *Charity and Children engaged in Navigation and Husbandry*, 1745 by John Michael Rysbrack (1694–1770)

**overleaf:
The Court Room**

Determined to make the most of the opportunity to show the public how high they could aim, the artists of the four large paintings chose biblical subjects that related to the work of the Hospital. The contribution of Joseph Highmore (1692–1780), *Hagar and Ishmael*, depicts the rescuing angel appearing to the destitute mother with her outcast child when they are on the point of death in the wilderness. James Wills (fl. 1740–77) chose a rather more obvious subject: *The Little Children brought before Christ.*

Francis Hayman (1708–76)
***The Finding of the Infant Moses in the Bulrushes*, 1746**
Exodus Chapter 2 describes how Moses' mother set her baby adrift in a basket in defiance of Pharaoh's edict that all male Hebrew children must be killed. Hayman depicts the moment when the child is discovered. At the urging of Moses' sister, who has watched to see what becomes of her brother, the mother is summoned by Pharaoh's daughter and ordered to foster the baby: 'Take this child away, and nurse it for me, and I will give thee thy wages.' The reference to the Hospital's system of placing their charges with wet-nurses is inescapable.

William Hogarth (1697–1764)
Moses Brought Before Pharaoh's Daughter, 1746
Hogarth chose to illustrate a later episode in the life of Moses, the moment when he is returned to Pharaoh's daughter, who intends to raise him as her own child—just as the Hospital received children back from their nurses. Hogarth's contemporary, the diarist George Vertue, commented: 'its Generally said and allowd that Hogarths peece gives most strikeing satisfaction & approbation'.

Roundels in The Court Room

Hung between the four large biblical paintings were landscapes and topographical paintings. Not all of these were ready in time for the public dinner, but all were installed by 1751. The landscapes were small round views of the Foundling Hospital and seven other London Hospitals, including Christ's (founded in 1552) and St George's (founded 1733). In giving these images such a prominent place in the decorative scheme of the Court Room, the Foundling Hospital was making a bold claim to equality with more venerable and well-established Hospitals. The 21-year-old Thomas Gainsborough (1727–88) contributed the view of the Charterhouse. The others were by Richard Wilson (1713–82) Edward Haytley (*fl.* 1740–61) and Samuel Wale (1721–86).

Not all the artists received commissions as a result of displaying their work in the Hospital. James Wills eventually gave up painting altogether and became a country curate, later complaining, 'If when I put up the Foundling Hospital picture there had been patrons, judges or lovers of the art, I need not have suffered this exile or have been under the necessity of resigning the art itself.' Some of the other artists, including Hogarth, had better luck. More importantly, it was out of the artists' annual meetings that the idea grew of holding an annual exhibition of British art—an idea that led eventually to the founding of the Royal Academy.

Thomas Gainsborough
(1727–88)
The Charterhouse,
1748

Richard Wilson
(1713–82)
*The Foundling
Hospital*, 1746

The Gerald Coke Handel Collection Exhibition Room.

One part of the fair copy of *The Messiah* bequeathed to the Foundling Hospital in Handel's will.

Second Floor

Handel and the Foundling Hospital

Handel's publisher, John Walsh, was elected as a governor of the Hospital in 1748, and it may be through him that Handel initially offered a performance of his music in 1749 to fund the completion of the Hospital's chapel. For this occasion he composed the anthem *Blessed are they that considereth the poor*, now popularly known as the Foundling Hospital Anthem. The event was a huge success, which attracted large numbers of the wealthy classes to take an interest in the Hospital and generated much-needed funds. The governors turned to Handel for a further concert the following year.

The performance of *Messiah* on 1 May 1750 was oversubscribed and double booked, to the extent that a further performance was arranged for a fortnight later for those who had missed the first concert. It was after these performances that the popularity of *Messiah*, which had been composed nine years earlier, became established; its first London performance in 1743 had been indifferently received. The 1750 performances were such a financial success for the Hospital, generating £1,000 from two performances alone, that an annual benefit performance of *Messiah* was agreed with Handel which continued until his death in 1759. Handel bequeathed a copy of the score and parts of *Messiah* to the Hospital in his will; these have been preserved by the charity and can now be seen alongside the will from Gerald Coke's collection in the Handel exhibition on the second floor of the Museum.

The Handel exhibition area includes both permanent and changing exhibitions, and also has some specially designed

School of Thomas Hudson
George Frideric Handel
(1701–1779)

"musical chairs", where visitors can sit and listen to a wide selection of Handel's works. The books accompanying each chair give more detail and background on the composer and the recordings than is possible on exhibit labels, and the central table with engraved timelines places Handel in a political, social, musical and cultural context.

The Gerald Coke Handel Collection

Gerald Coke started to collect Handel material in the 1930s, choosing Handel after a brief period collecting Mozart (which proved too expensive), because as he said "virtually the whole of Handel's output was first published in England, and was still obtainable at a reasonable price". The collection grew rapidly to include such significant items as Handel's will, autograph letters, rare first editions and contemporary portraits, as well as, in later years, the whole of William Smith's Handel collection along with twenty-four boxes of Smith's working papers relating to various publications. Coke died in 1990 and in 1995 the collection was

John Dunthorne
The Concert Party

Left: Handel's Will

Right: Modello for Handel's monument by Roubiliac in Westminster Abbey.

offered to the State under the Acceptance in Lieu scheme; in 2008 it was formally allocated to the Foundling Museum.

The core of the Coke collection is the significant number of manuscripts and printed editions from the eighteenth century; together with a large number of prints, drawings and engravings. Perhaps the most important is Handel's will and four codicils, displayed in the gallery, and there are also letters and several manuscripts annotated by Handel. Unique items include the Shaftesbury manuscripts, purchased in 1987 from the descendants of the 4th Earl of Shaftesbury, who was a contemporary of Handel, and correspondence of Handel, Charles Jennens and Charles Burney. Other rare items include the programme from the first *Messiah* performance and the first edition of the *Songs in Messiah.* There are around 300 manuscript scores in the collection, chiefly from the eighteenth century. Complementing Coke's collection is a number of items from the Foundling Hospital, including the score and parts of *Messiah* bequeathed to the Hospital in Handel's will.

The major art works include oil paintings of Handel's librettist Charles Jennens, Richard Leveridge, John Beard and J.C. Smith the younger, among others, and a large number of prints and engravings of contemporary composers and performers. The ceramic and bronze busts of the composer include a large black plaster bust after Roubiliac, which was rescued from the fire at the music publishers Novello's. Also by Roubiliac is a terracotta modello for the monument to the composer in Westminster Abbey, and smaller items include a Bow porcelain model of the singer Kitty Clive and numerous medals and tokens issued for various

Oratorio singers at the Drury Lane Theatre, c1814 John Nixon (1760–1818) Pen and ink with wash

festivals from the eighteenth to the twentieth centuries.

The library includes items relating to Handel's circle and his surroundings, and there are many manuscripts and printed works by contemporaries of Handel, as well as a significant collection of art works. Handel's singers, patrons, friends and surroundings are well represented, so that the collection is now a rich resource for eighteenth-century musical studies. There are periodicals and collected editions, together with modern scores and literature, and a large collection of ephemera, comprising concert tickets, playbills, newspaper cuttings, programmes and advertisements, from the eighteenth century to the present day, only a small number of which can be displayed at any one time.

Research facilities

The Coke collection has its own staff, and the reading room is normally open three days a week (Wednesday to Friday) for research by appointment. The exhibition area is open from Tuesday to Sunday during Museum opening hours. handel@foundlingmuseum.org.uk

GERALD COKE
Handel
COLLECTION

THE *foundling* MUSEUM

020 7841 3606

Messiah an Oratorio

Mr Wass

Further reading

Jamila Gavin, *Coram Boy*, Egmont Books, London 2000

Ruth K. McClure, *Coram's Children. The London Foundling Hospital in the eighteenth century*, New Haven and London: Yale University Press, 1981

R. H. Nichols and F. A. Wray, *The History of the Foundling Hospital*, London: Oxford University Press/Humphrey Milford, 1935

Benedict Nicolson, *The Treasures of the Foundling Hospital*, Oxford: Clarendon Press, 1972

Christine Oliver and Peter Aggleton, *Coram's Children. Growing up in the care of the Foundling Hospital 1900–1955*, London: Coram Family, 2000

Gillian Wagner, *Thomas Coram, Gent*, Boydell Press, 2004

Martha Jocelyn, *A Home for Foundlings,* Tundra Books, 2005

Gillian Pugh, *London's Forgotten Children, Thomas Coram and the Foundling Hospital*, The History Press, 2007

Gerald Coke, *Tercentenary of the birth of George Frederic Handel: the Gerald Coke Handel Collection exhibition*, Jenkyn Place, Bentley, Hampshire, 1985

Donald Burrows (ed), Gerald Coke Handel Foundation, *Handel's will: facsimiles and commentary*, London, 2009

WE WILL MOREOVER,
that all persons who shall subscribe
and pay to the said Corporation
to the amount of twenty pounds or more,
or of forty shillings or more annually,
shall have free liberty
to inspect the said hospital

- from the George II Charter establishing
A Hospital for the Maintenance and Education of
Exposed and Deserted Young Children (1739)

William MacMillan RA
(1887–1977)
***Thomas Coram*, 1963**
Statue outside
40 Brunswick Square